SCHOLASTIC discover more™

Animal Faces

By Penelope Arlon and
Tory Gordon-Harris

Discover even more with your free digital companion book.

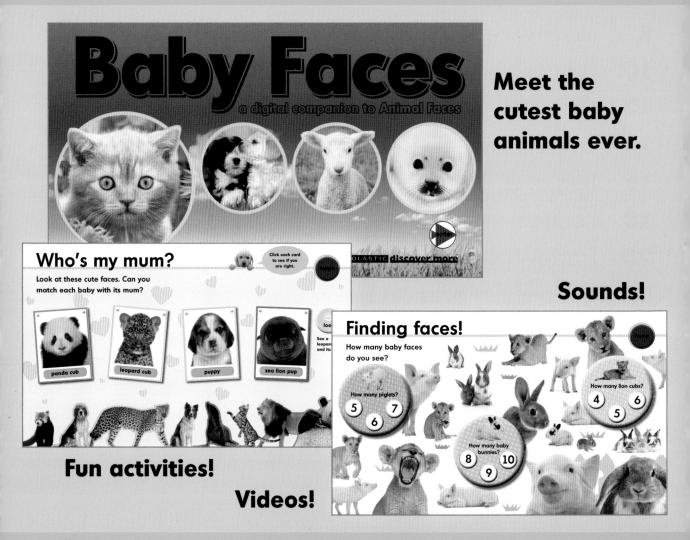

Meet the cutest baby animals ever.

Sounds!

Fun activities!

Videos!

To download your free digital book, visit **www.scholastic.com/discovermore**

Enter this special code: RMAFC6HCG427

Contents

Natural History Consultant: Kim Dennis-Bryan, PhD

Copyright © 2015 by Scholastic Inc.

All rights reserved. Published by Scholastic Inc., *Publishers since 1920*.
SCHOLASTIC, SCHOLASTIC DISCOVER MORE™, and associated logos are trademarks and/or registered trademarks of Scholastic Inc.

No part of this publication may be reproduced, stored in a retrieval system, or transmitted in any form or by any means, electronic, mechanical, photocopying, recording, or otherwise, without written permission of the publisher. For information regarding permission, write to Scholastic Inc., Attention: Permissions Department, 557 Broadway, New York, NY 10012.

Distributed in the UK by
Scholastic UK Ltd
Westfield Road
Southam, Warwickshire
England CV47 0RA

Library of Congress Cataloging-in-Publication Data Available

ISBN 978 1407 14898 4

10 9 8 7 6 5 4 3 2 1   15 16 17 18 19

Printed in Malaysia   108
First edition 2015

Scholastic is constantly working to lessen the environmental impact of our manufacturing processes.
To view our industry-leading paper procurement policy, visit www.scholastic.com/paperpolicy

tarsier

snake

Face to face

Look in the mirror. Your face is amazing! These animals have amazing faces, too! Their features are useful.

eagle

A giant panda's furry face keeps it warm.

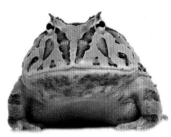

A frog has a wide mouth. It swallows prey whole!

A ladybird's antennae are used to smell.

A lizard's bulging eyes help it spot prey.

Huge ears help bats hear well in the dark.

Some animal faces can show off, too!

Senses

Most animals have five senses. They use their senses to find food and keep safe. Animals sense with their ears, eyes, mouths, and even whiskers.

A cat senses a tasty mouse across the room. It uses its sharp eyesight and hearing.

Sixth sense

Some animals have extra senses. The pit viper has pits next to its eyes. It can sense the heat of yummy prey.

3. Hearing
Big ears listen for danger – such as cats!

2. Sight
The eyes watch for danger.

4. Touch
Whiskers help feel around in dark places.

1. Taste
The tongue tastes food to find out if it's good to eat.

5. Smell
The nose sniffs for food.

Extreme senses

Some animals have senses that are very powerful. Meet some sense superstars.

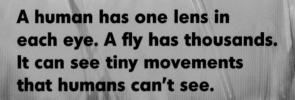

A human has one lens in each eye. A fly has thousands. It can see tiny movements that humans can't see.

Super senses

A dog's nose is 10,000 times better at smelling than yours!

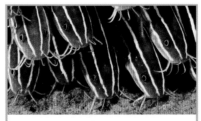

A catfish's barbels, or whiskers, can taste water to find prey.

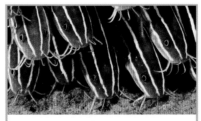

A tarsier's face is almost all eyes! Big eyes see in the dark.

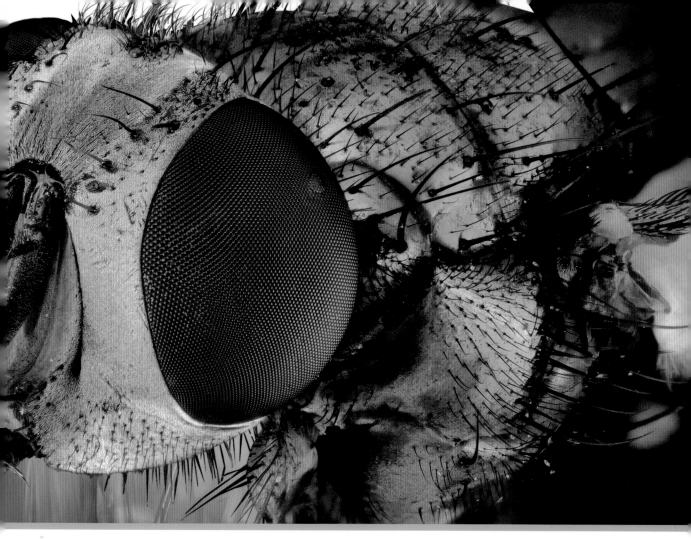

A shark's nostrils can smell blood nearly 1.6 km (1 mile) away.

An elephant's trunk can sense elephants 3.2 km (2 miles) away.

An owl's ears can hear a mouse's heartbeat 9 m (30 ft) away!

Using colour

There's more to colour than just beauty. A colourful face can scare, hide, or say a big "Hi!" to other animals!

The brighter a male mandrill's nose, the more important he is.

This bird uses its colourful crest to show off!

A wasp's stripes warn animals that it may sting.

A chameleon can change its skin colour to show that it is calm or upset.

Reef fish hide in coral reefs that are as colourful as they are.

This frog's bright blue colour shows that it is poisonous.

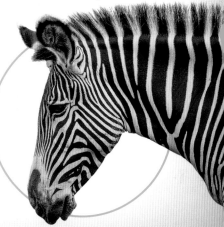

A zebra's stripes confuse animals that are chasing it.

Mammals

rhino

All mammals have hair. Hair helps keep them warm, and it can also protect them!

This horn is made of the same stuff that hair is!

Orang-utans are very hairy. But important males, like this one, have big bald cheeks.

12

bison

bobcat

hedgehog

giraffe

Thick hair is warm!

Whiskers can help feel in the dark.

Spines are stiff, prickly hairs.

Eyelashes keep dirt and dust away from the eyes.

Brilliant birds

Birds have beaks.
Their funny-looking
beaks have
many uses.

toucan

This pelican can
hold lots of fish
in its long beak.

flamingo

turkey

egret

hoopoe

macaw

finch

Birds use their beaks to keep their feathers clean. This is called preening.

Some birds touch beaks to show that they like each other.

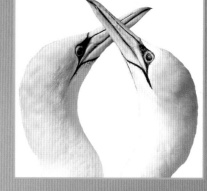

Vultures have sharp beaks. They can tear through meat.

woodpecker

kingfisher

blackbird

Bug eyes

Up close, bugs have very strange faces. Their faces are perfect for how they eat, hunt, and behave.

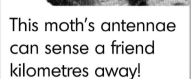

This moth's antennae can sense a friend kilometres away!

An army ant's sharp jaws tear into attackers.

These butterflies don't have mouths. Their long tongues sip liquid.

Most spiders have eight eyes. This jumping spider can see in all directions at the same time!

Reptiles rule!

Some reptiles have faces that are designed for killing. You need to be quick to avoid these predators!

A crocodile's mouth is filled with over 60 sharp teeth. Just one SNAP can kill!

This snake's sharp fangs inject a poison into its prey.

Snakes taste the air with their forked tongues to find prey.

A chameleon shoots out its long, sticky tongue. Watch out, flies!

Reptiles can be
gentle. Caimans
carry their babies
in their mouths.

Froggy faces

Frogs have bulging eyes and wide mouths. Some can be heard croaking 1.6 km (1 mile) away!

Frogs and toads are amphibians. They live on land and in water.

Frogs can hide in water and peep out above it with just their eyes showing.

Frogs blink to swallow food. Their eyeballs help push food down.

This frog has a throat sac like a balloon. It can croak extra loudly!

Frogs breathe through their skin as well as their mouths.

Underwater eyes

Some of the strangest faces
in the world belong to
animals in the ocean.

grouper

butterfly
fish

sea horse

boxfish

cuttlefish

A scallop has over 40 blue eyes along the edges of its shell.

A hammerhead shark has eyes at the edges of its head. It can see all around to spot prey.

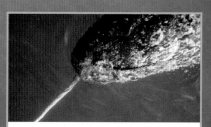

A narwhal's huge tooth can feel changes in the water.

A crab has antennae that can taste and smell to find food.

When a lion wants to scare another animal, it opens its mouth and roars.

Scary!

Keep away from me! Animals sometimes use their faces to frighten other animals.

A cobra rears its head. It fans out its skin to scare animals away.

A frilled lizard spreads out its neck frill and hisses loudly.

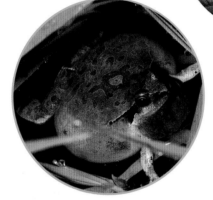

This frog has big fake eyes on its bottom! Creepy!

A puffer fish can blow up its body. Now it's too big to eat!

That's weird!

Check out these crazy faces!
Are they even from our planet?

This shrimp's eyes are on stalks. They can move in different directions at the same time.

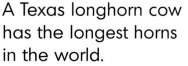

A Texas longhorn cow has the longest horns in the world.

A thorny devil has spikes all over its body, even on its face.

An elephant's huge trunk can smell water 19 km (12 miles) away!

This hummingbird's beak is longer than the rest of its body.

A star-nosed mole uses its strange nose to feel around.

A bumblebee's hairy eyes feel the wind. This helps it fly in the right direction.

Baby faces

This seal turns black as it grows up.

Some animal babies don't look at all like their parents! Looking different often keeps them safe. All these babies change as they grow.

A penguin chick has fluffy down. As it gets older, it grows waterproof feathers.

A caterpillar can't fly. It eats and eats before turning into a butterfly.

This baby seal is born with white fur. It can hide in the snow.

This baby snake is yellow. It can hide on the forest floor. The adult is green so that it can hide in trees.

A tadpole is born in water. It changes shape and grows legs as it becomes a frog.

Glossary

amphibian
An animal that lives in water when it is young, and both in water and on land when it is an adult. Frogs and toads are amphibians.

antenna
A sticklike feelers on an insect's head that it uses to sense the world around it. The plural of *antenna* is *antennae*.

bald
Without feathers or hair.

barbel
A feeler that grows from the mouth or jaw of a fish.

beak
A bird's hard, pointed jaw.

coral reef
A strip of coral just below the surface of the sea. Coral is a material made up of the skeletons of tiny sea creatures.

crest
A tuft of feathers on the top of a bird's head.

down
Soft, fluffy feathers.

fake
Not true or real.

fang
A long, pointed hollow tooth that some snakes use to inject poison.

feather
One of the soft, warm parts that cover a bird's body.

forked tongue
A tongue that is split into two at the tip.

hiss
To make a sound like a long drawn-out s. Snakes hiss.

lens
The part of an eye that helps the eye to focus.

predator
An animal that hunts and eats other animals.

preening
Arranging and cleaning feathers with a beak.

prey
An animal that is hunted by another animal as food.

reptile
An animal that lays eggs and is covered in scales. Crocodiles, chameleons and snakes are reptiles.

senses
One of the powers that an animal uses to learn about its surroundings. Senses include sight, hearing, touch, smell, and taste.

spine
A hard, pointed part that sticks out from an animal's body. Hedgehogs have spines.

tadpole
A young frog that lives in water and has a tail. When it is very young, it has no legs.

whisker
A long, stiff hair that grows near an animal's mouth. Cats and mice have whiskers.

Index

Credits